the best of
Hank Williams

T0028159

Cover photo courtesy of the Country Music Hall of Fame and Museum
Used by permission

ISBN 978-0-634-00218-2

HAL•LEONARD®
CORPORATION
7777 W. BLUEMOUND RD. P.O. BOX 13819 MILWAUKEE, WI 53213

Visit Hal Leonard Online at
www.halleonard.com

STRUM AND PICK PATTERNS

This chart contains the suggested strum and pick patterns that are referred to by number at the beginning of each song in this book. The symbols ⊓ and ∨ in the strum patterns refer to down and up strokes, respectively. The letters in the pick patterns indicate which right-hand fingers plays which strings.

p = **thumb**
i = **index finger**
m = **middle finger**
a = **ring finger**

For example; Pick Pattern 2
is played: thumb - index - middle - ring

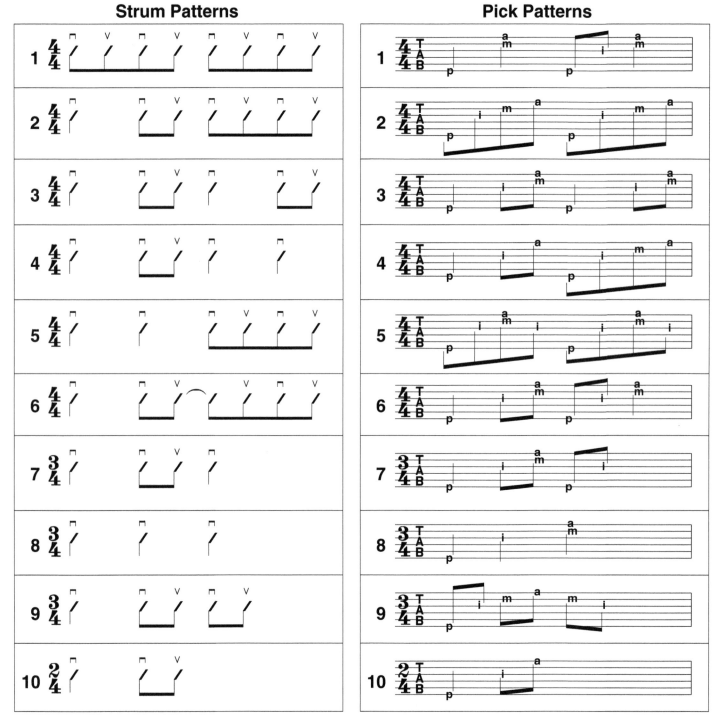

You can use the 3/4 Strum or Pick Patterns in songs written in compound meter (6/8, 9/8, 12/8, etc.). For example, you can accompany a song in 6/8 by playing the 3/4 pattern twice in each measure. The 4/4 Strum and Pick Patterns can be used for songs written in cut time (¢) by doubling the note time values in the patterns Each pattern would therefore last two measures in cut time

Honky Tonkin'

Words and Music by Hank Williams

Strum Pattern: 3, 4
Pick Pattern: 1

Additional Lyrics

2. When you and your baby
   Have a fallin' out,
   Just call me up sweet mama,
   And we'll go steppin' out, and we'll go...

3. We're goin' to the city,
   To the city fair.
   If you go to the city,
   You will find me there, and we'll go...

The Alabama Waltz

Words and Music by Hank Williams

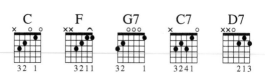

Strum Pattern: 7
Pick Pattern: 9

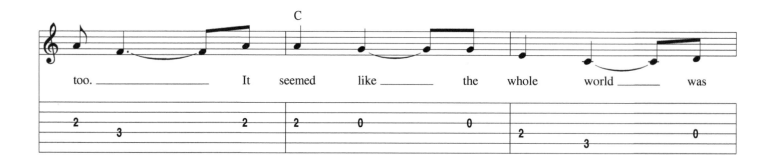

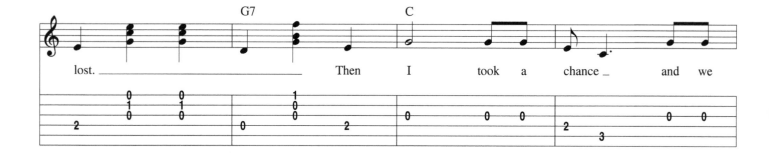

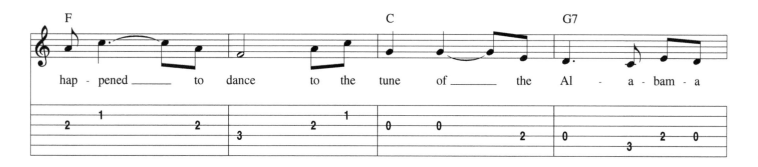

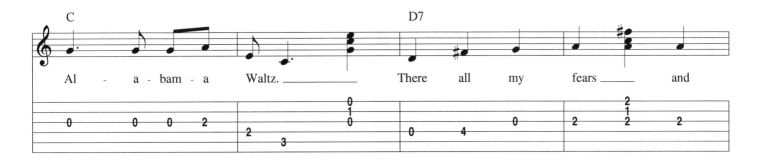

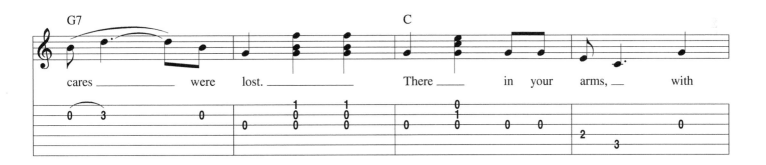

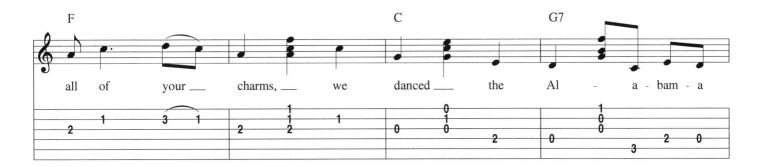

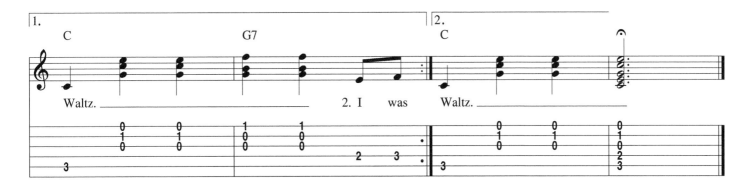

Baby, We're Really in Love

Words and Music by Hank Williams

run a-round in cir-cles, ___ and turn in fire a-larms. _____ I'm nut-ty as a
See Additional Lyrics

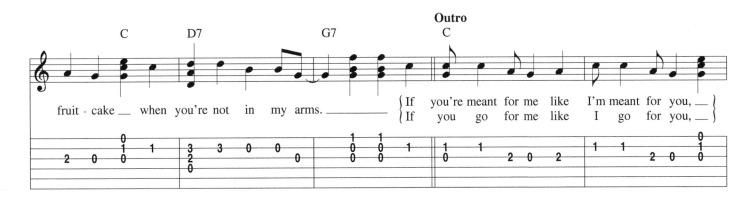

fruit-cake ___ when you're not in my arms. _____

{ If you're meant for me like I'm meant for you, ___ }
{ If you go for me like I go for you, ___ }

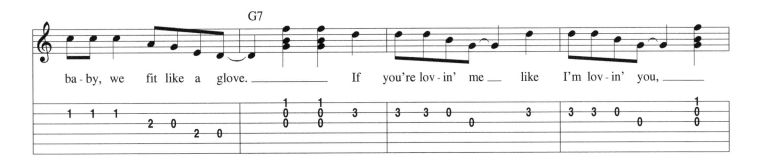

ba-by, we fit like a glove. _____ If you're lov-in' me ___ like I'm lov-in' you, _____

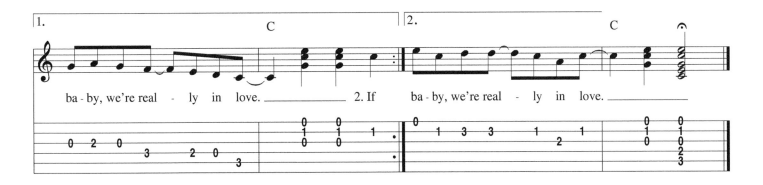

ba-by, we're real - ly in love. _____ 2. If   ba-by, we're real - ly in love. _____

Additional Lyrics

2. If you're lovin' me like I'm lovin' you,
   Baby, we're really in love.
   If you're countin' on me like I'm countin' on you,
   Cupid just gave us a shove.
   If you're dreamin' of me like I'm dreamin' of you,
   Then I know what you're dreamin' of.
   If you're lovin' me like I'm lovin' you,
   Baby, we're really in love.

Bridge My folks think I've gone crazy, and I don't feel too sure.
   And yet there's nothin' wrong with me that weddin' bells won't cure.

The Blues Come Around

Words and Music by Hank Williams

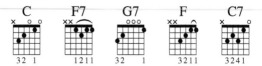

Strum Pattern: 3, 4
Pick Pattern: 1, 6

Verse
Moderately

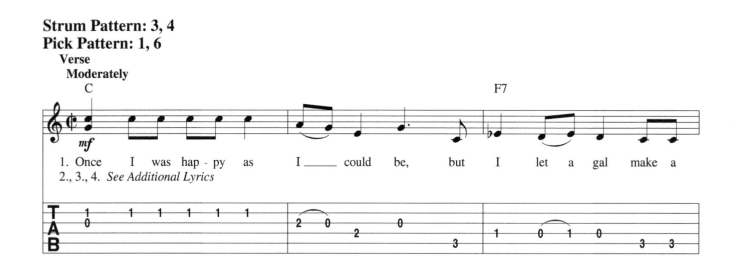

1. Once I was hap - py as I ___ could be, but I let a gal make a
2., 3., 4. *See Additional Lyrics*

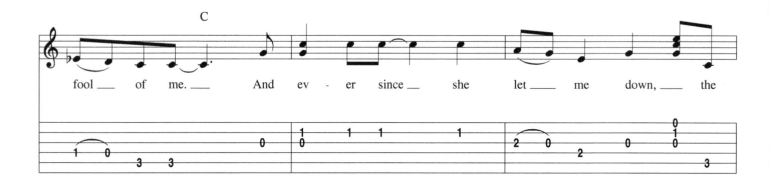

fool ___ of me. ___ And ev - er since ___ she let ___ me down, ___ the

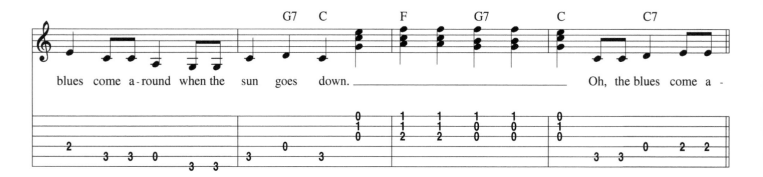

blues come a - round when the sun goes down. ___ Oh, the blues come a -

Chorus

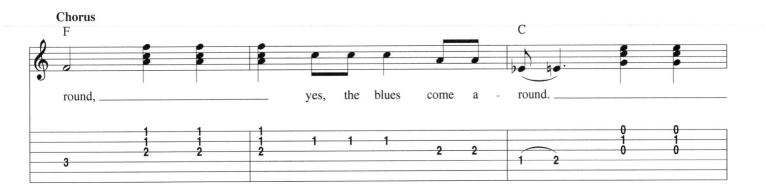

round, _____ yes, the blues come a - round. _____

_____ Lawd, the blues come a - round ev - 'ry eve - nin' when the sun ___ goes

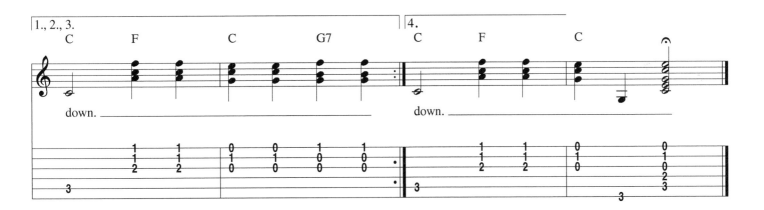

down. _____ down. _____

Additional Lyrics

2. Long as the sun is in the sky,
   These dog-gone blues never make me cry.
   But ever since she left this town,
   The blues come around when the sun goes down.

3. I built my castles very high,
   And then she went and said goodbye.
   And ever since she tore 'em down,
   The blues come around when the sun goes down.

4. Once she called me all her own,
   But now she's gone and I'm alone.
   And ev'ry evenin' I'm sorrow bound,
   'Cause the blues come around when the sun goes down.

Calling You

Words and Music by Hank Williams

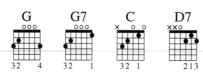

Strum Pattern: 3, 4
Pick Pattern: 2, 5

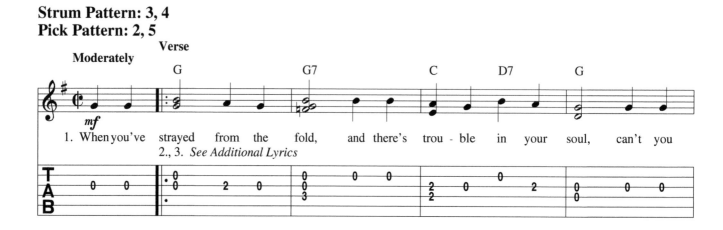

1. When you've strayed from the fold, and there's trou - ble in your soul, can't you
2., 3. *See Additional Lyrics*

hear the bles - sed Sav - iour call - ing you? _____ When your

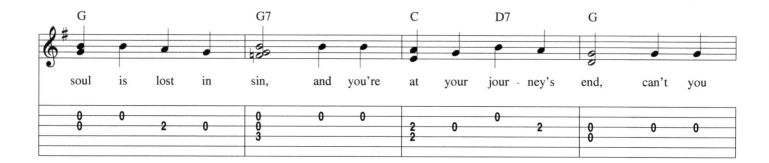

soul is lost in sin, and you're at your jour - ney's end, can't you

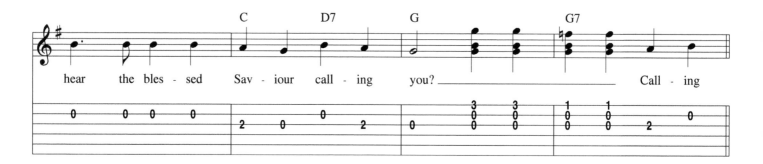

hear the bles - sed Sav - iour call - ing you? _____ Call - ing

Chorus

you, _____ call - ing you, _____ can't you

hear the bles - sed Sav - iour call - ing you? _____ He will

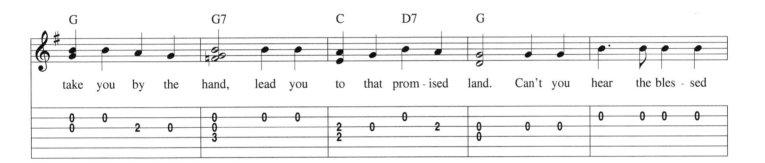

take you by the hand, lead you to that prom - ised land. Can't you hear the bles - sed

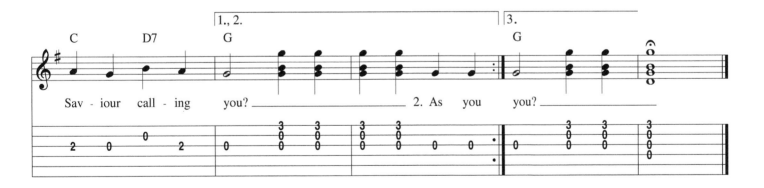

Sav - iour call - ing you? _____ 2. As you you? _____

Additional Lyrics

2. As you journey day by day, and temptation comes your way,
   Can't you hear the blessed Saviour calling you?
   If you follow in His light, He will always guide you right,
   Can't you hear the blessed Saviour calling you?

3. When your soul is burdened down, and your friends cannot be found,
   Can't you hear the blessed Saviour calling you?
   If you follow Him each day, He will brighten up your way,
   Can't you hear the blessed Saviour calling you?

Cold, Cold Heart

Words and Music by Hank Williams

Strum Pattern: 4
Pick Pattern: 1

Verse
Moderately

1. I tried so hard, my dear, to show that you're my ev-'ry dream. _____ Yet
3. *See Additional Lyrics*

you're a-fraid each thing I do is just some e-vil scheme. _____ A

mem-'ry from your lone-some past keeps us so far a-part. _____ Why

can't I free your doubt-ful mind and melt your cold, cold heart? _____ 2. An-oth-er love be-
4. *See Additional Lyrics*

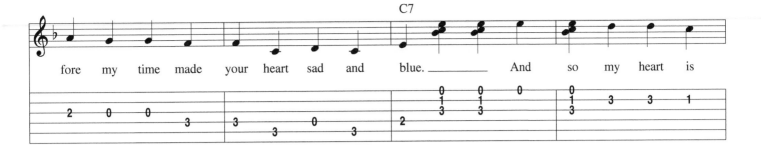

fore my time made your heart sad and blue._____ And so my heart is

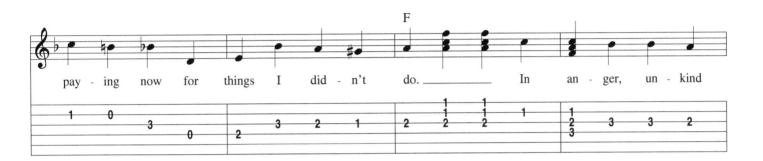

pay - ing now for things I did - n't do._____ In an - ger, un - kind

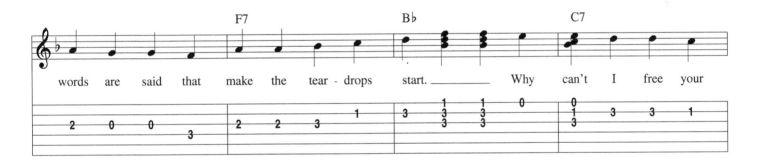

words are said that make the tear - drops start._____ Why can't I free your

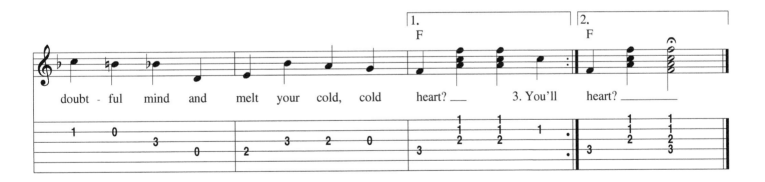

doubt - ful mind and melt your cold, cold heart? __ 3. You'll heart? _____

Additional Lyrics

3. You'll never know how much it hurts
   To see you sit and cry.
   You know you need and want my love
   Yet you're afraid to try.
   Why do you run and hide from life?
   To try it just ain't smart.
   Why can't I free your doubtful mind
   And melt your cold, cold heart?

4. There was a time when I believed
   That you belonged to me.
   But now I know your heart is shackled
   To a memory.
   The more I learn to care for you,
   The more we drift apart.
   Why can't I free your doubtful mind
   And melt your cold, cold heart?

Countryfied

Words and Music by Hank Williams

Additional Lyrics

2. Now country ham and turnip greens,
   That's somethin' fit to eat.
   And I just don't feel comf'table
   'Less I'm ridin' on a wagon seat.
   God gave me land to make my bread
   And air to breath so free.
   Go on and call me countryfied,
   You shore ain't sland'rin' me.

3. Just one thing more I'll be forced to say
   Before I head for home.
   I'm proud to be a country man
   'Cause that's where I belong.
   And if I treat my neighbor right,
   And to my God I'm true,
   There's one thing that I surely know,
   I'll get to heaven just as quick as you.

Dear Brother

Words and Music by Hank Williams

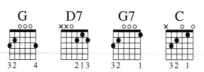

Strum Pattern: 8
Pick Pattern: 8

Verse
Moderately Slow

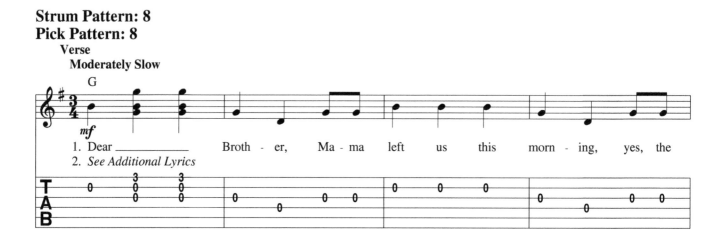

1. Dear _____ Broth - er, Ma - ma left us this morn - ing, yes, the
2. *See Additional Lyrics*

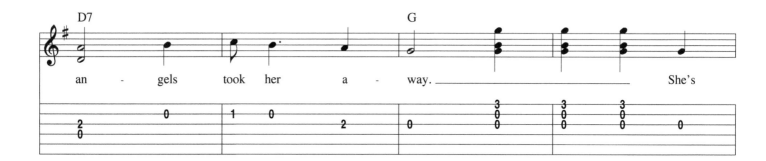

an - gels took her a - way. _____ She's

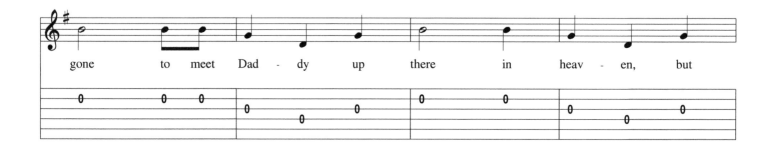

gone to meet Dad - dy up there in heav - en, but

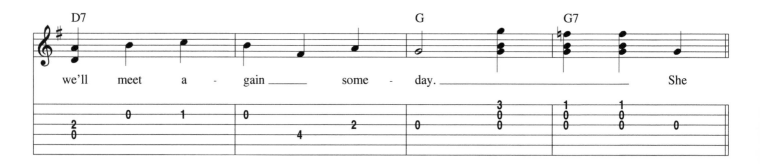

we'll meet a - gain _____ some - day. _____ She

Chorus

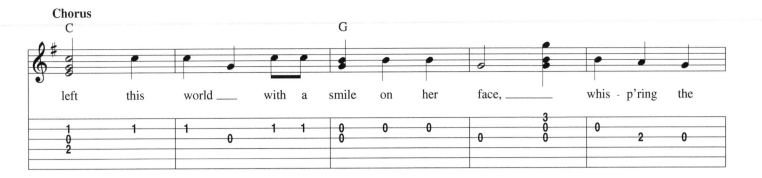

left this world ___ with a smile on her face, _____ whis - p'ring the

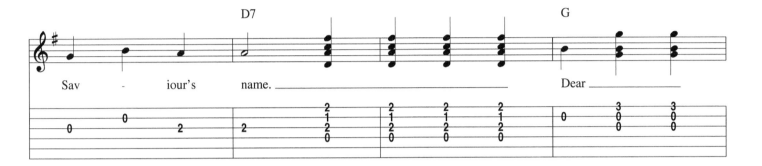

Sav - iour's name. _____ Dear _____

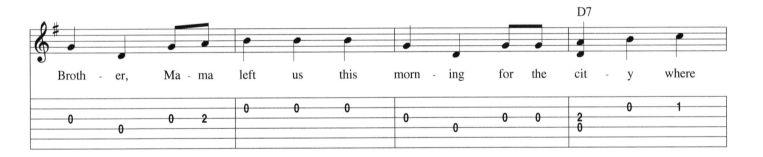

Broth - er, Ma - ma left us this morn - ing for the cit - y where

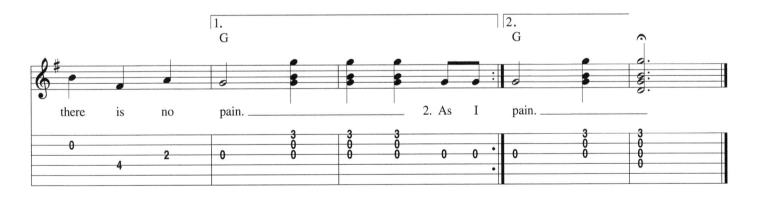

there is no pain. _____ 2. As I pain. _____

Additional Lyrics

2. As I stood by her bedside those last few moments,
   I lived my childhood again.
   I tho't of you, Brother, and of the old homestead,
   And my tears they fell like rain.

Help Me Understand

Words and Music by Hank Williams

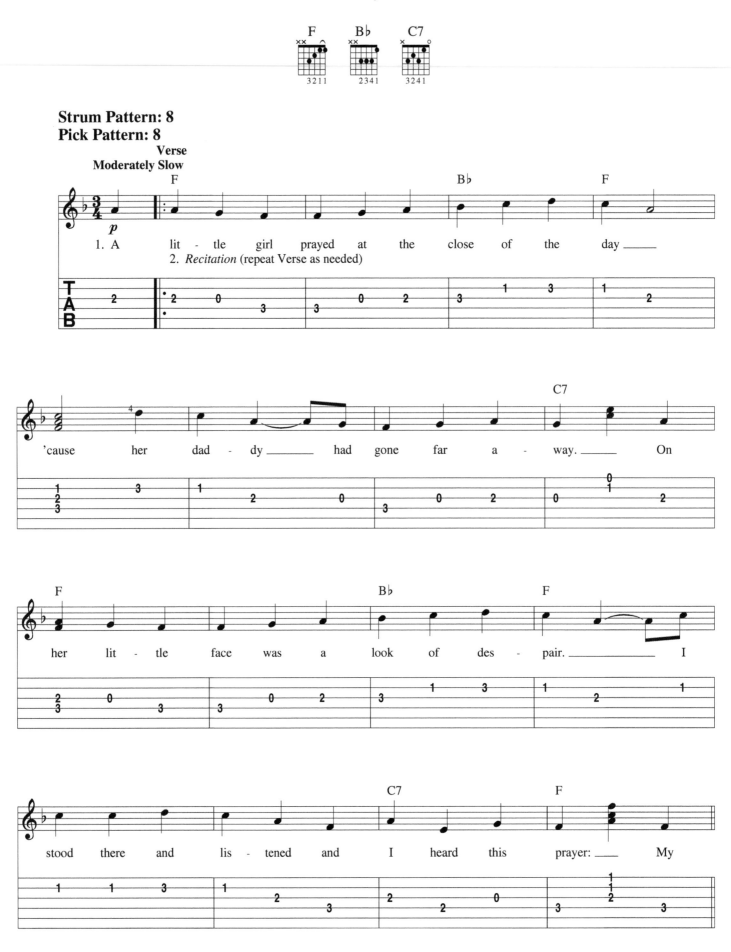

Chorus

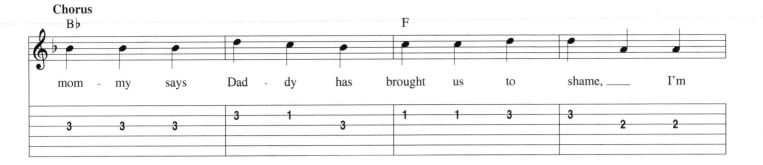

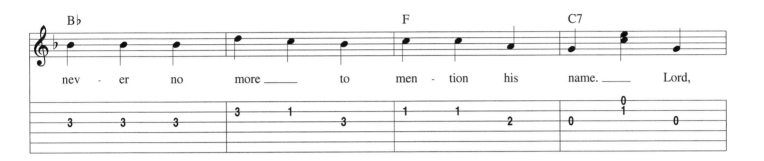

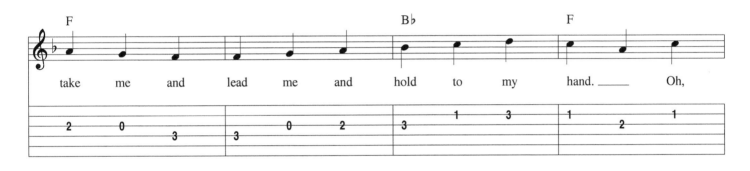

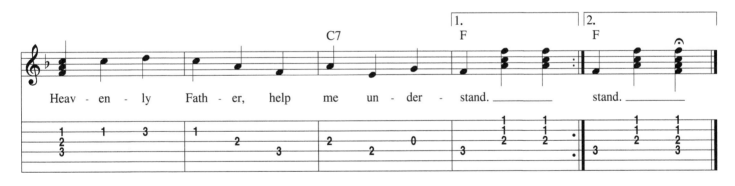

Additional Lyrics

RECITATION

2. You know, friends, I wonder how many homes are broken tonight—just how many tears are shed
By some little word of anger that never should have been said.
I'd like to tell you a story of a family I once knew.
We'll call them Mary and William and their little daughter, Sue.
Mary was just a plain mother, and Bill—well, he was the usual dad,
And they had their family quarrels, like everyone else—but neither one got mad.
Then one day something happened—it was nothing, of course,
But one word led to another, and the last word led to a divorce.
Now here were two grown-up people who failed to see common sense.
They strengthened their own selfish pride—at little Sue's expense.
You know, she didn't ask to be brought into this world—to drift from pillar to post,
But a divorce never stops to consider the one it hurts the most.
There'd be a lot more honest lovin' in this wicked world today
If just a few parted parents could here little Sue say:

Hey, Good Lookin'

Words and Music by Hank Williams

Strum Pattern: 3, 4
Pick Pattern: 4, 5

1. Hey, hey, _____ good look-in', what - cha got cook-in'?
2. *See Additional Lyrics*

How's a - bout cook - in' some - thin' up ___ with me? _____

Hey _____ sweet ba - by, don't _____ you think may - be

we could find us a brand new rec - i - pe? _____ I got a
See Additional Lyrics

Bridge

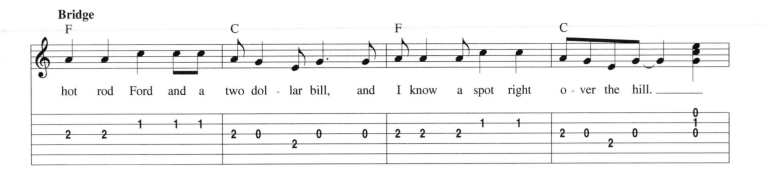

hot rod Ford and a two dol - lar bill, and I know a spot right o - ver the hill. _____

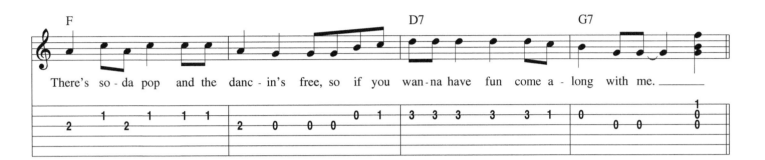

There's so - da pop and the danc - in's free, so if you wan-na have fun come a - long with me. _____

Outro

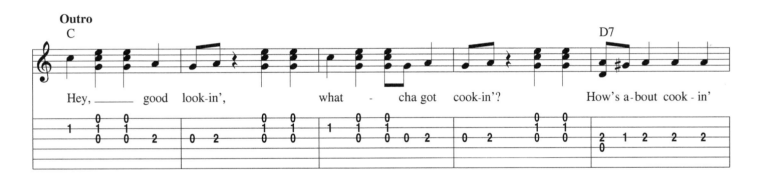

Hey, _____ good look-in', what - cha got cook-in'? How's a-bout cook - in'

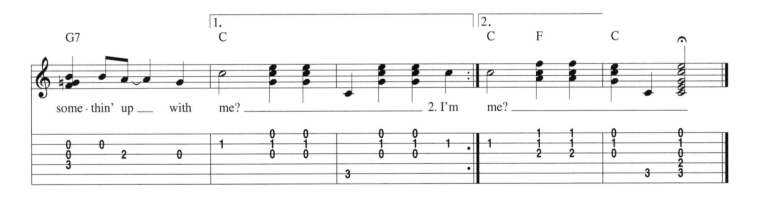

some - thin' up ___ with me? _____ 2. I'm me? _____

Additional Lyrics

2. I'm free and ready
   So we can go steady.
   How's about savin' all your time for me?
   Hey sweet lookin',
   I know I've been tooken.
   How's about keepin' steady company?

Bridge I'm gonna throw my date book over the fence,
   And find me one for five or ten cents.
   I'll keep it 'til it's covered with age,
   'Cause I'm writin' your name down on ev'ry page.

Honky Tonk Blues

Words and Music by Hank Williams

Strum Pattern: 3, 4
Pick Pattern: 1, 3

Verse
Moderately Slow

1. I left my home _ down on a ru - ral route _ and told my folks _ I'm go - in'
3., 5. *See Additional Lyrics*

step - pin' out _ to get the honk - y tonk blues, _____ the jump - in'

honk - y tonk blues. _____ Lord I got 'em, _____

_____ I got the honk - y tonk blues. _____

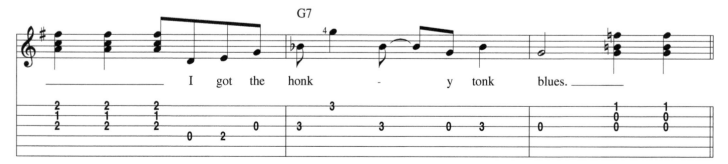

Verse

2., 6. I went to ___ a dance, wore out my shoes, _ woke up this morn - in' wish - in'
4. *See Additional Lyrics*

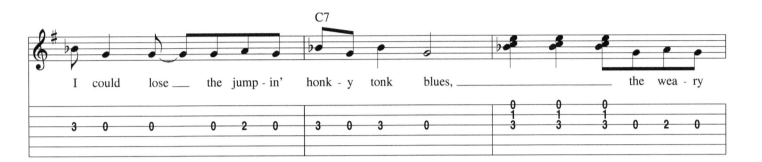

I could lose ___ the jump - in' honk - y tonk blues, _____ the wea - ry

honk - y tonk blues. _____ Lord I'm suf - ferin' _____ with the

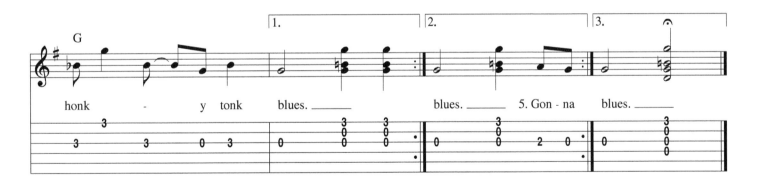

honk - y tonk blues. _____ blues. _____ 5. Gon - na blues. _____

Additional Lyrics

3. I stopped into ev'ry place in town.
   This city life has really got me down.
   I got the honky tonk blues.
   I got the honky tonk blues.
   Lord, I'm sufferin' with the honky tonk blues.

4. When I get home again to Ma and Pa,
   I know they're gonna lay down the law
   About the honky tonk blues,
   The jumpin' honky tonk blues.
   Lord, I'm sufferin' with the honky tonk blues.

5. Gonna tuck my worries underneath my arm,
   And get right back to my pappy's farm,
   And leave the honky tonk blues.
   Forget the honky tonk blues.
   I don't want to be bothered with the honky tonk blues.

A House Without Love

Words and Music by Hank Williams

Strum Pattern: 4
Pick Pattern: 1

Bridge

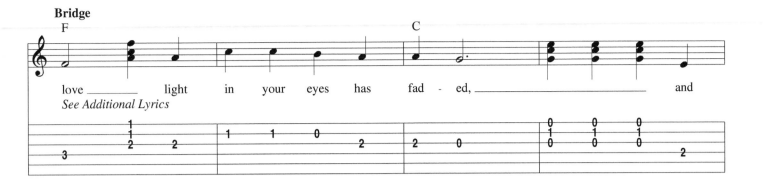

love _____ light in your eyes has fad - ed, _____ and
See Additional Lyrics

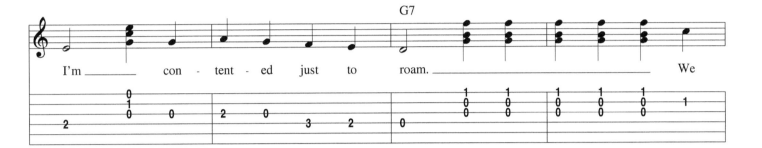

I'm _____ con - tent - ed just to roam. _____ We

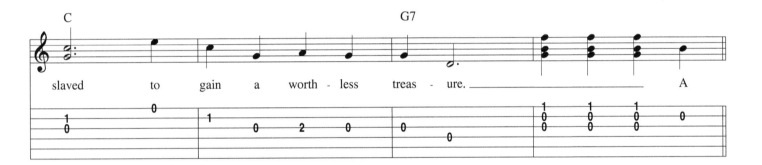

slaved to gain a worth - less treas - ure. _____ A

Outro

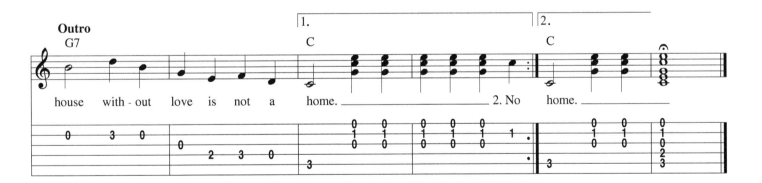

house with - out love is not a home. _____ 2. No home. _____

Additional Lyrics

2. No matter where our footsteps wander,
   I know we'll both be all alone
   With the pride that came between us.
   A house without love is not a home.

Bridge The simple things have gone forever.
   We wanted wealth to call our own,
   And now we've reached the hour of parting.

I Can't Get You Off of My Mind

Words and Music by Hank Williams

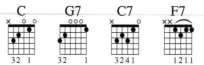

Strum Pattern: 3, 4
Pick Pattern: 1, 4

Intro
Moderately

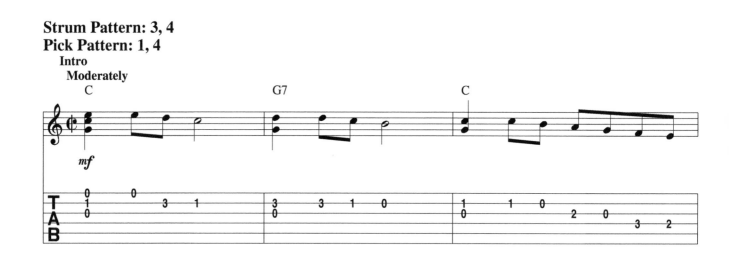

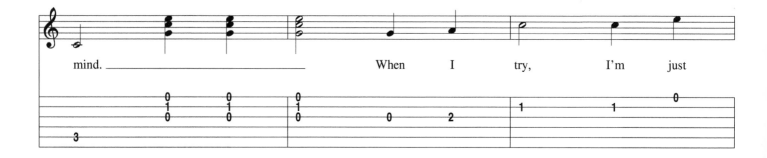

wast - ing my time. _____ Lord I've

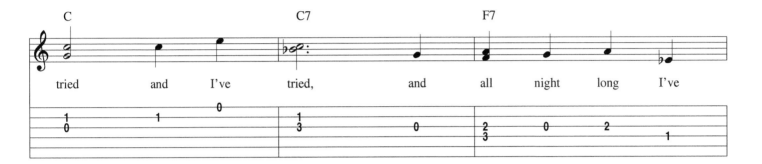

tried and I've tried, and all night long I've

cried, but I can't get you off _____ of my

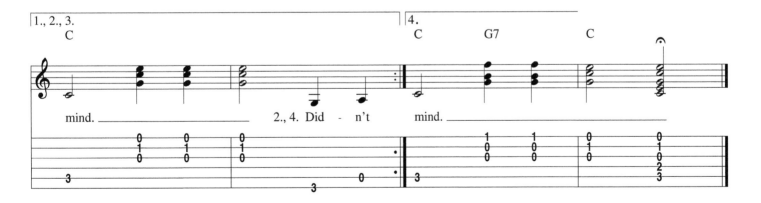

mind. _____ 2., 4. Did - n't mind. _____

Additional Lyrics

2., 4. Didn't think you would leave me behind,
But I guess you're the two-timin' kind.
Do you think that it's smart
To jump from heart to heart,
When I can't get you off of my mind?

3. You believe that a new love is blind,
So you fool ev'ry true love you find.
You've got stars in your eyes,
But they can't hide the lies.
Oh, I can't get you off of my mind.

I Can't Help It
(If I'm Still in Love With You)

Words and Music by Hank Williams

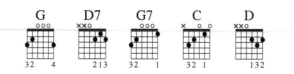

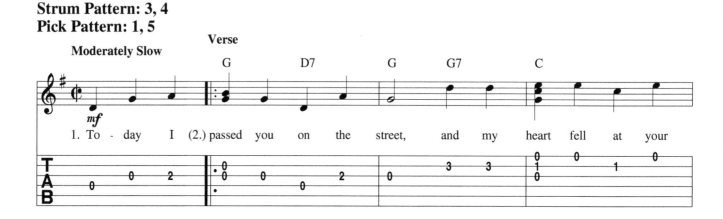

Strum Pattern: 3, 4
Pick Pattern: 1, 5

Moderately Slow

Verse

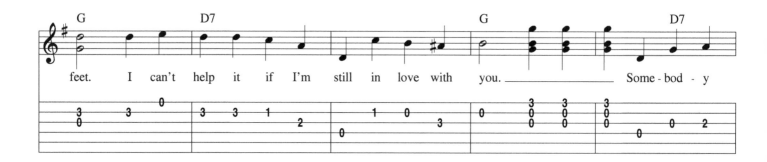

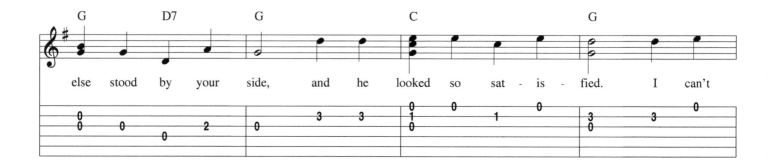

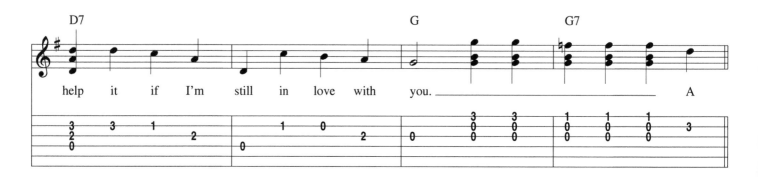

Bridge

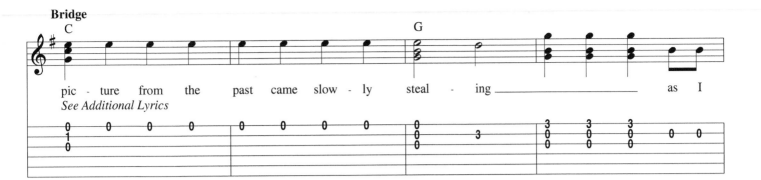

pic - ture from the past came slow - ly steal - ing _____ as I
See Additional Lyrics

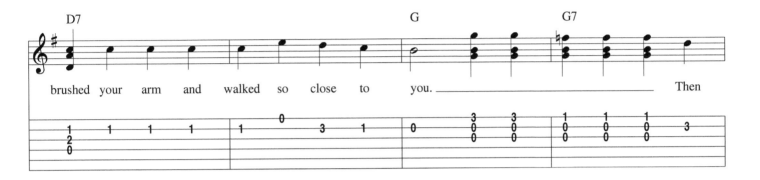

brushed your arm and walked so close to you. _____ Then

Outro

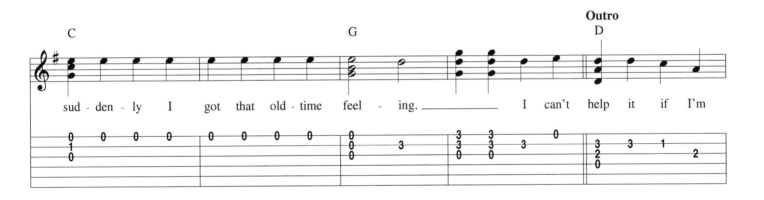

sud - den - ly I got that old - time feel - ing. _____ I can't help it if I'm

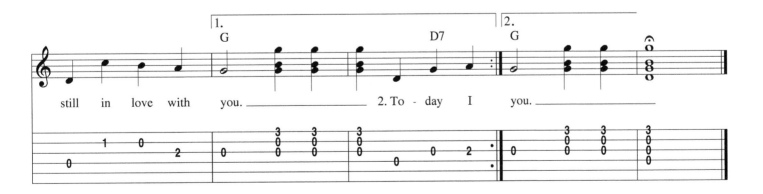

still in love with you. _____ 2. To - day I you. _____

Additional Lyrics

Bridge It's hard to know another's lips will kiss you,
And hold you just the way I used to do.
Oh, heaven only knows how much I miss you.

I Saw the Light

Words and Music by Hank Williams

Chorus

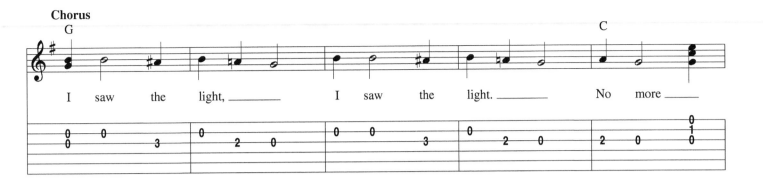

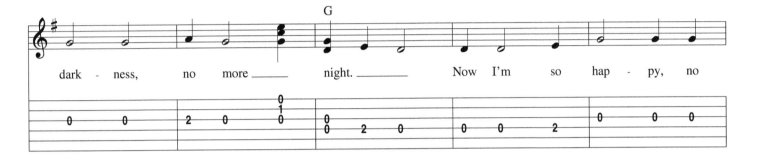

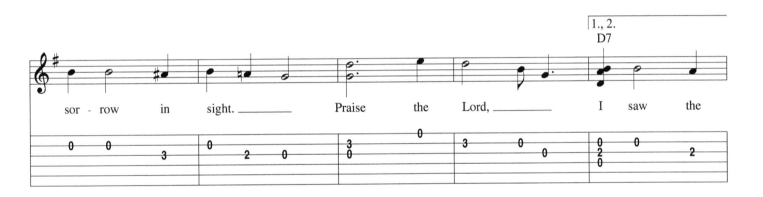

Additional Lyrics

2. Just like a blind man, I wandered along.
   Worries and fears I claimed for my own.
   Then like the blind man that God gave back his sight,
   Praise the Lord, I saw the light.

3. I was a fool to wander and stray.
   Straight is the gate and narrow the way.
   Now I have traded the wrong for the right.
   Praise the Lord, I saw the light.

I'm a Long Gone Daddy

Words and Music by Hank Williams

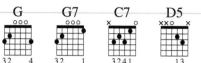

Strum Pattern: 2, 5
Pick Pattern: 1, 2

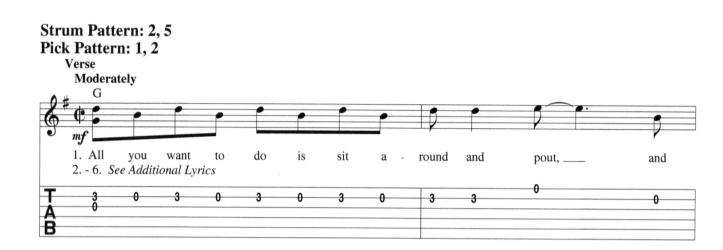

1. All you want to do is sit a - round and pout, ___ and
2. - 6. *See Additional Lyrics*

now I got e - nough and so I'm step - pin' out. ___ I'm

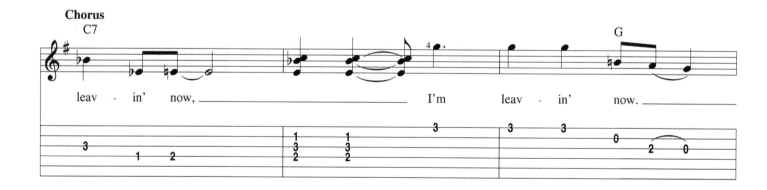

leav - in' now, _____ I'm leav - in' now. ___

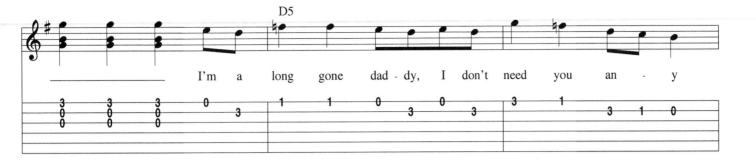

I'm   a   long   gone   dad - dy,   I   don't   need   you   an - y

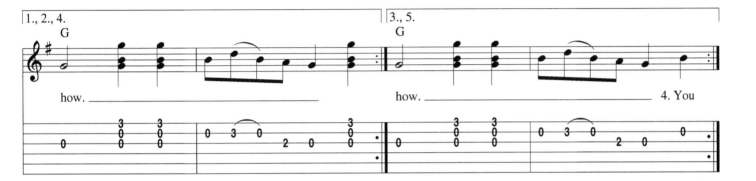

how. _____   how. _____   4. You

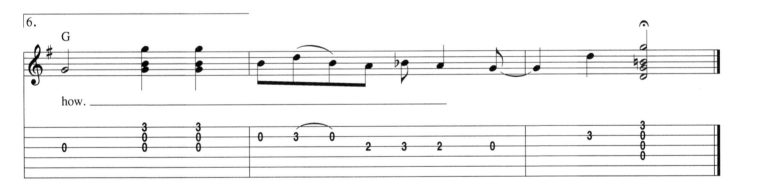

how. _____

Additional Lyrics

2. I've been in the doghouse for so dog-gone long,
   That when I get a kiss I think that something's wrong.

3. I'll go find a gal that wants to treat me right,
   You go get yourself a man that wants to fight.

4. You start your jaws a-waggin' and they never stop,
   You never shut your mouth until I blow my top.

5. I remember back when you were nice and sweet,
   Now things have changed, you'd rather fight than eat.

6. I'm gonna do some ridin' on the midnight train,
   I'm taking ev'rything except my ball and chain.

I'm So Lonesome I Could Cry

Words and Music by Hank Williams

Strum Pattern: 8
Pick Pattern: 8

Verse
Moderately

1. Hear _____ that lone - some whip - poor will, he sounds _____ too blue _____ to fly. _____ The mid - night train is whin - ing low, I'm so lone - some I could _ cry. _____ 2. I've cry. _____ 3. Did you

cry. _____

Additional Lyrics

2. I've never seen a night so long,
   When time goes crawling by.
   The moon just went behind a cloud
   To hide its face and cry.

3. Did you ever see a robin weep
   When leaves began to die?
   That means he's lost the will to live,
   I'm so lonesome I could cry.

4. The silence of a falling star
   Lights up a purple sky.
   And as I wonder where you are,
   I'm so lonesome I could cry.

Kaw-Liga

Words by Fred Rose
Music by Hank Williams

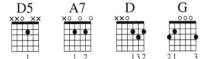

Strum Pattern: 1
Pick Pattern: 1

Intro
Moderately

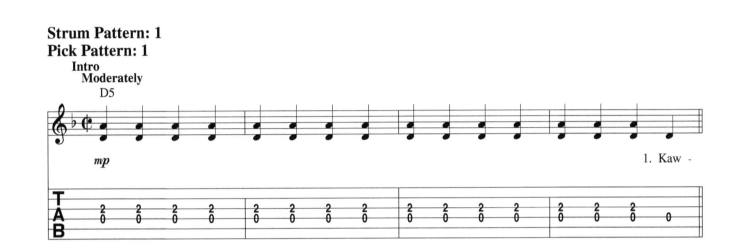

mp

1. Kaw -

Verse

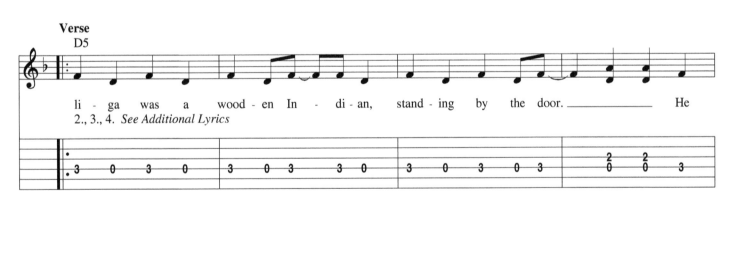

li - ga was a wood - en In - di - an, stand - ing by the door. _____ He
2., 3., 4. *See Additional Lyrics*

fell in love with an In - di - an maid - en o - ver in the an - tique store. _____ Kaw -

li - ga, _____ just

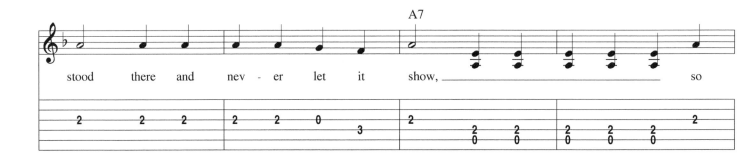

stood there and nev - er let it show, _____ so

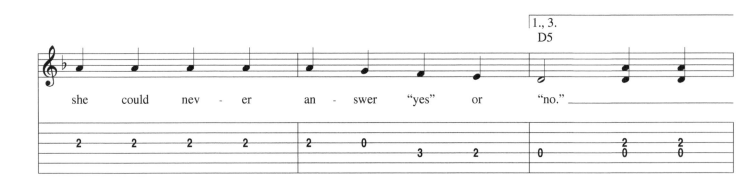

she could nev - er an - swer "yes" or "no." _____

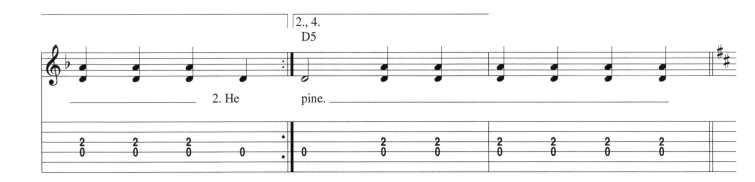

_____ 2. He pine. _____

Chorus

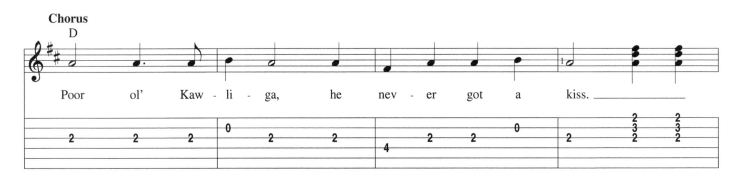

Poor ol' Kaw - li - ga, he nev - er got a kiss. _____

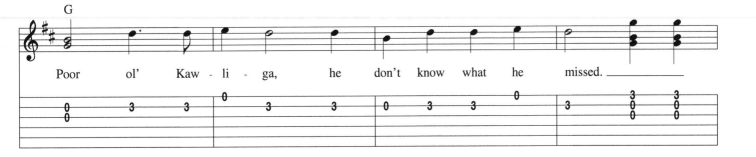

Poor ol' Kaw-li-ga, he don't know what he missed. _____

Is it an-y won-der that his face is red? Kaw -

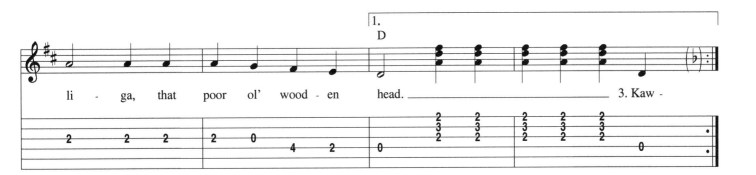

1.

li-ga, that poor ol' wood-en head. _____ 3. Kaw -

2.

head. _____

Additional Lyrics

2. He always wore his Sunday feathers and held a tomahawk.
   The maiden wore her beads and braids and hoped someday he'd talk.
   Kaw-liga, stubborn to ever show a sign,
   Because his heart was made of knotty pine.

3. Kaw-liga was a lonely Indian, never went nowhere.
   His heart was set on the Indian maiden with the coal black hair.
   Kaw-liga stood there and never let it show,
   So she could never answer "yes" or "no."

4. And then one day a wealthy customer bought the Indian maid.
   And took her, oh, so far away but ol' Kaw-liga stayed.
   Kaw-liga stands there as lonely as can be,
   And wishes he was still an old pine tree.

If You'll Be a Baby
(To Me)

Words and Music by Hank Williams

Strum Pattern: 4
Pick Pattern: 5

Verse

Moderately

1. I'll be your ba - by, _____ and I don't mean may - be, _____ if

2. *See Additional Lyrics*

you'll be a ba - by to me. _____ I'll be your

dar - lin', _____ and there'll be no quarrel - in', _____ if

you'll be a ba - by to me. _____ 'Cause

Bridge

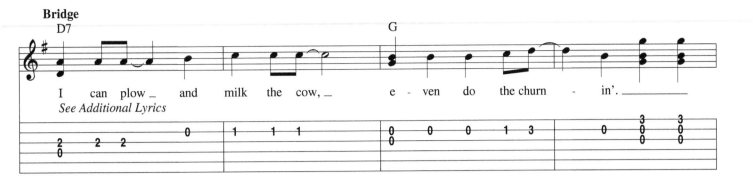

I can plow __ and milk the cow, __ e - ven do the churn - in'. _____
See Additional Lyrics

You just look __ thru your cook - book __ and keep the home fires burn - in.' 'Cause

Outro

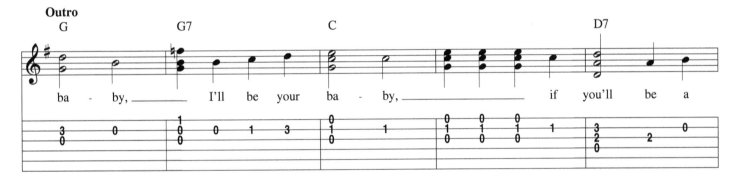

ba - by, _____ I'll be your ba - by, _____ if you'll be a

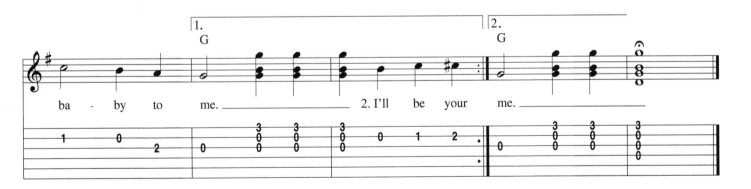

ba - by to me. _____ 2. I'll be your me. _____

Additional Lyrics

2. I'll be your honey, let you spend my money,
If you'll be a baby to me.
I'll be your dandy, and I'll bring you candy,
If you'll be a baby to me.

Bridge 'Cause I can work and pay the bills,
And make believe it thrills me.
You can bake a choc'late cake,
I'll eat it if it kills me.

Jambalaya
(On the Bayou)

Words and Music by Hank Williams

Strum Pattern: 4
Pick Pattern: 1

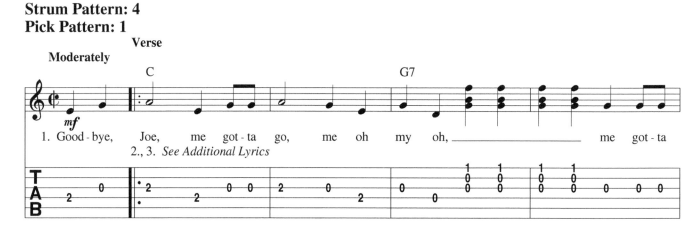

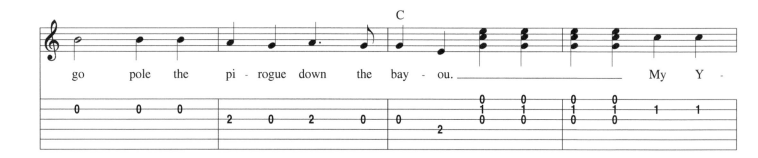

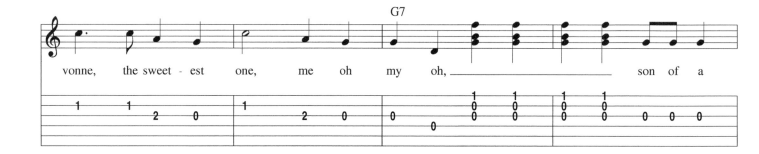

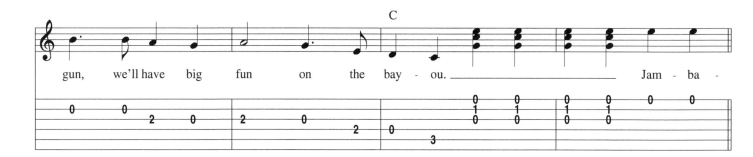

Chorus

la - ya and a craw - fish pie and fil - let gum - bo, _____ 'cause to -

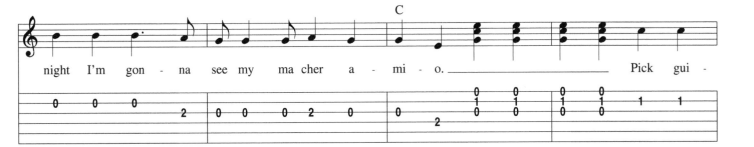

night I'm gon - na see my ma cher a - mi - o. _____ Pick gui -

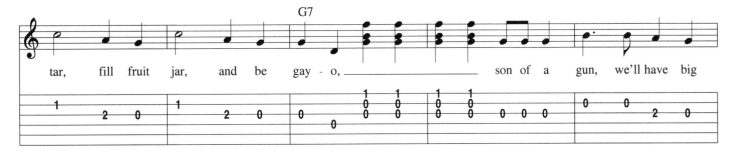

tar, fill fruit jar, and be gay - o, _____ son of a gun, we'll have big

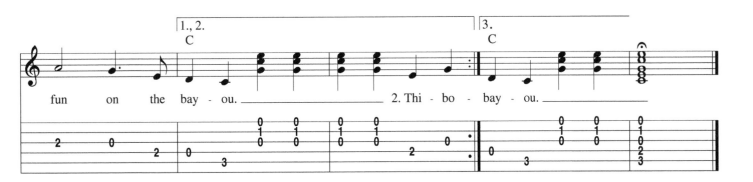

fun on the bay - ou. _____ 2. Thi - bo - bay - ou. _____

Additional Lyrics

2. Thibodaux, Fontaineaux, the place is buzzin',
   Kin folk come to see Yvonne by the dozen.
   Dress in style and go hog wild, me oh my oh,
   Son of a gun, we'll have big fun on the bayou.

3. Settle down far from town, get me a pirogue,
   And I'll catch all the fish in the bayou.
   Swap my mon to buy Yvonne what we need-o,
   Son of a gun, we'll have big fun on the bayou.

The Little House We Built

Words and Music by Hank Williams

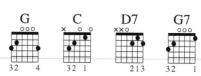

Strum Pattern: 3, 4
Pick Pattern: 1

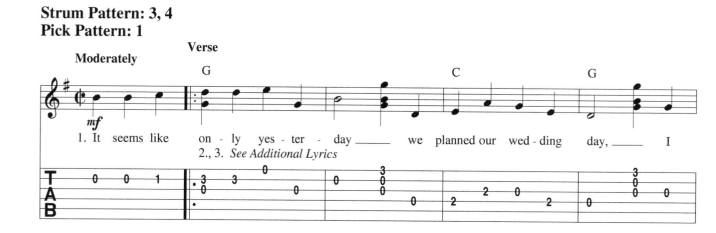

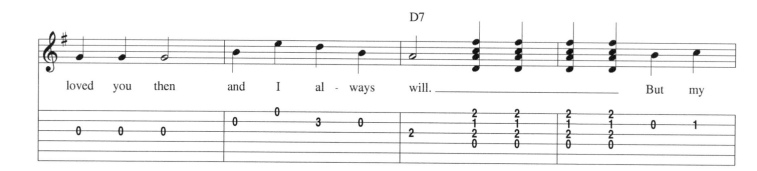

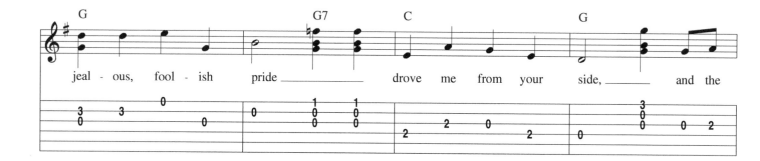

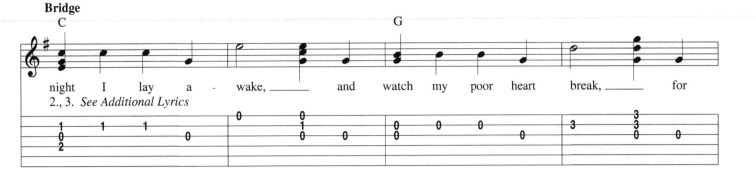

night   I   lay   a - wake, _____   and   watch   my   poor   heart   break, _____   for

2., 3. See Additional Lyrics

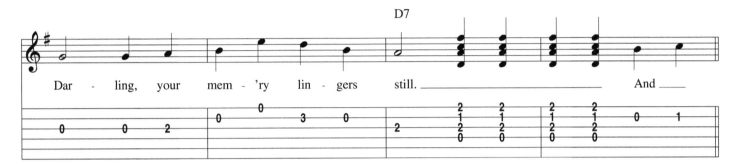

Dar - ling,   your   mem - 'ry   lin - gers   still. _____   And ____

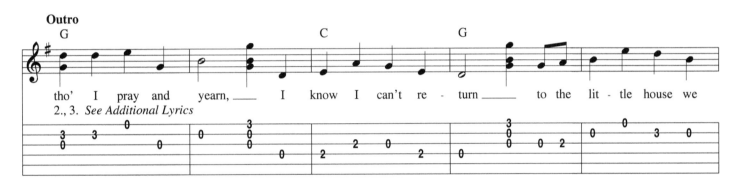

Outro

tho'   I   pray   and   yearn, ____   I   know   I   can't   re - turn _____   to the   lit - tle   house   we

2., 3. See Additional Lyrics

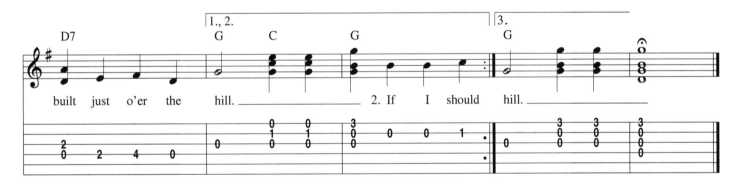

built   just   o'er   the   hill. _____   2. If   I   should   hill. _____

Additional Lyrics

2. If I should pass you on the street,
   I know I couldn't speak,
   To see you would make my poor heart chill.
   For you'll welcome me no more,
   'Cause lies have locked the door
   To the little house we built just o'er the hill.

3. I would give my life tonight,
   Again to hold you tight,
   I'm lonely as a whippoor will.
   Tho' her love for me has gone,
   She won't ever be alone
   In the little house we built just o'er the hill.

Bridge 2. So cry, oh lying heart, you know you made us part,
           You cheated and now you'll pay the bill.

Bridge 3. Each time I hear her name, I bow my head in shame,
           For God only knows how I feel.

Outro 2. She won't meet you at the gate,
          For you there's only hate
          In the little house we built just o'er the hill.

Outro 3. And until He calls for me,
          I'll live in memory
          In the little house we built just o'er the hill.

Long Gone Lonesome Blues

Words and Music by Hank Williams

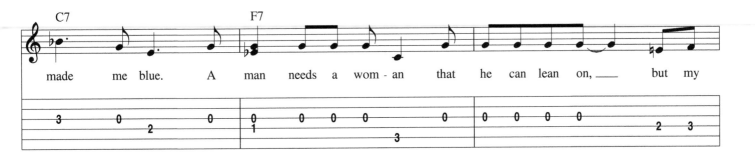

made   me   blue.   A   man   needs   a   wom-an   that   he   can   lean   on, ___   but   my

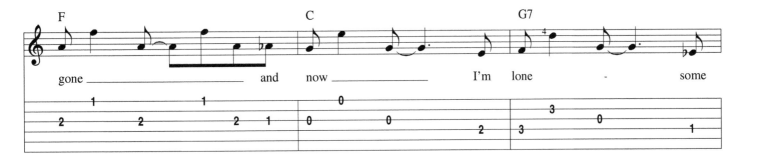

lean - in' post ___ is done left ___ and gone.   She's ___   long _____

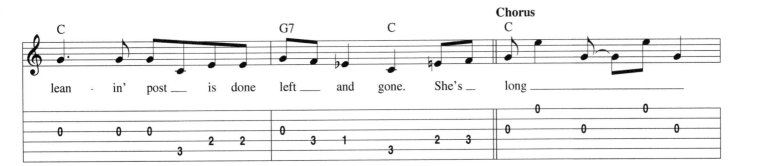

gone _____   and   now _____   I'm   lone   -   some

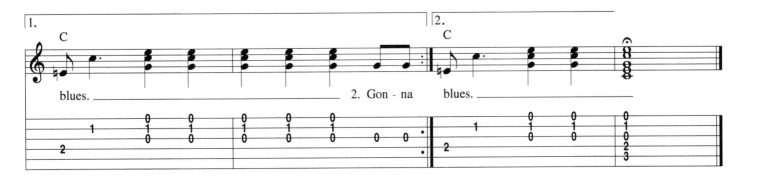

blues. _____   2. Gon - na   blues. _____

Additional Lyrics

2. Gonna find me a river, one that's cold as ice.
   When I find me that river, Lawd, I'm gonna pay the price.
   Oh, Lawd, I'm goin' down in it three times, but I'm only comin' up twice.

Pre-Chorus She told me on a Sunday she was checkin' me out.
   Along about Monday she was nowhere about,
   And here it is Tuesday, ain't had no news.
   Got them "gone" but not forgotten blues.

A Mansion on the Hill

Words by Fred Rose
Music by Hank Williams

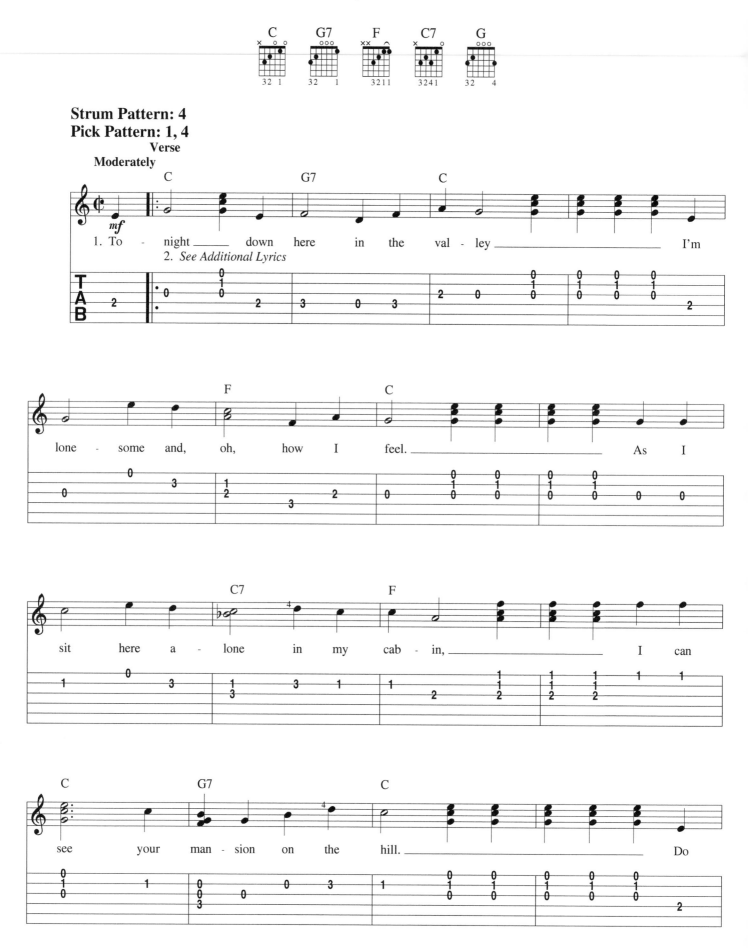

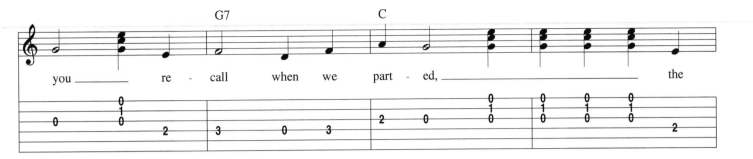

you _____ re - call when we part - ed, _____ the

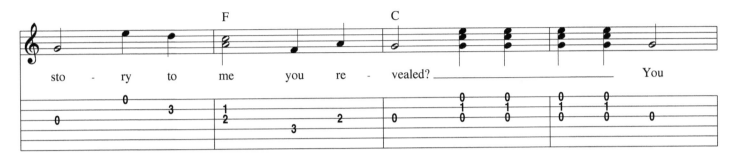

sto - ry to me you re - vealed? _____ You

said you could live with - out love, Dear _____ in you love - less

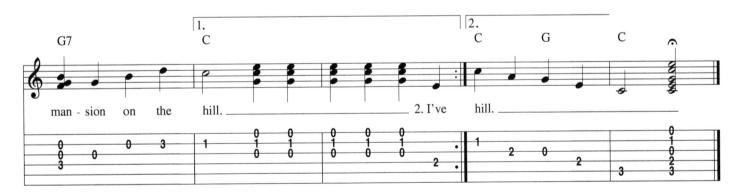

man - sion on the hill. _____ 2. I've hill. _____

Additional Lyrics

2. I've waited all through the years, love,
   To give you a heart true and real.
   'Cause I know you're living in sorrow
   In your loveless mansion on the hill.
   This light shines bright from your window,
   The trees stand so silent and still.
   I know you're alone with your pride, Dear,
   In your loveless mansion on the hill.

Mind Your Own Business

Words and Music by Hank Williams

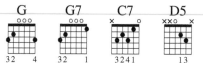

Strum Pattern: 3
Pick Pattern: 4

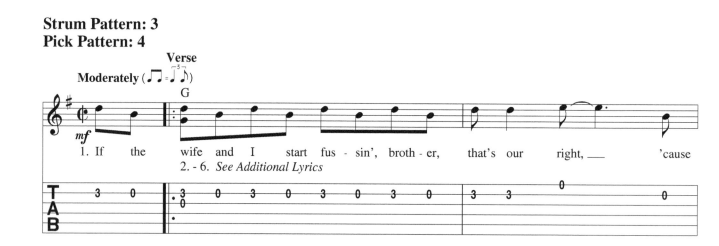

1. If the wife and I start fus - in', broth - er, that's our right, ___ 'cause
2. - 6. *See Additional Lyrics*

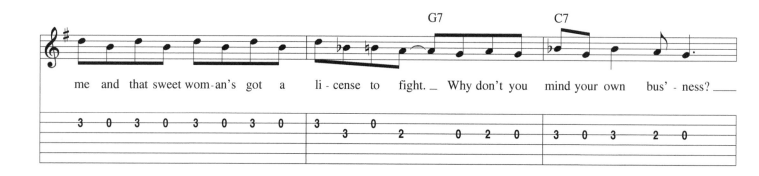

me and that sweet wom-an's got a li - cense to fight. __ Why don't you mind your own bus' - ness? ___

___ Mind your own bus' - ness. _____ 'Cause if you

Additional Lyrics

2. Oh, the woman on our party line's a nosey thing,
   She picks up her receiver when she knows it's my ring.
   Why don't you mind you own bus'ness? Mind your own bus'ness.
   Well if you mind your bus'ness then you won't be mindin' mine.

3. I got a little gal that wears her hair up high,
   The boys all whistle at her ev'ry time she walks by.
   Why don't you mind your own bus'ness? Mind your own bus'ness.
   Well if you mind your bus'ness then you won't be mindin' mine.

4. If I want to honky tonk around 'til two or three,
   Now brother, that's my headache, don't you worry 'bout me.
   Why don't you mind your own bus'ness? Mind your own bus'ness.
   'Cause if you mind your bus'ness you'll stay busy all the time.

5. I might tell a lot of stories that may not be true,
   But I can get to heaven just as easy as you.
   Why don't you mind your own bus'ness? Mind your own bus'ness.
   Well if you mind your bus'ness then you won't be mindin' mine.

6. Mindin' other people's bus'ness seems to be high-tone,
   But I got all that I can do just mindin' my own.
   Why don't you mind your own bus'ness? Mind your own bus'ness.
   Well if you mind your bus'ness you'll stay busy all the time.

Moanin' the Blues

Words and Music by Hank Williams

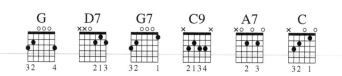

Strum Pattern: 3, 4
Pick Pattern: 1

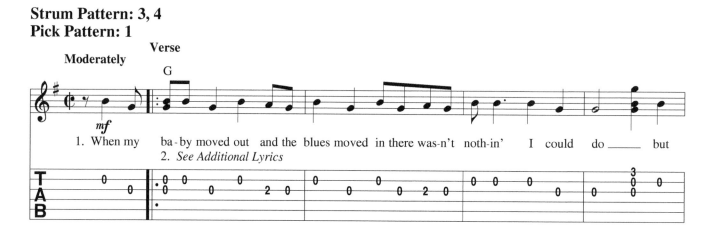

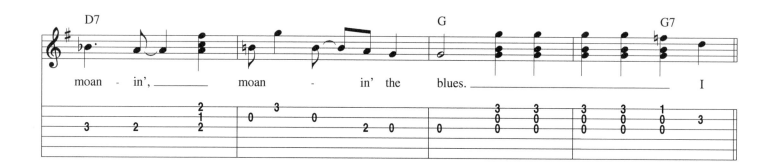

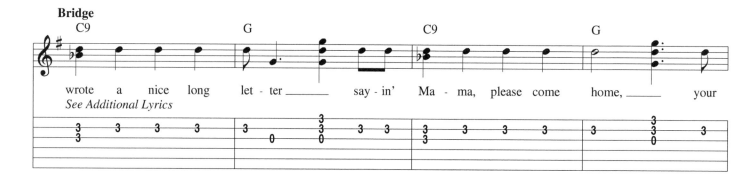

dad - dy is ___ lone - some and all I do ___ is moan. ___ I've been

Outro

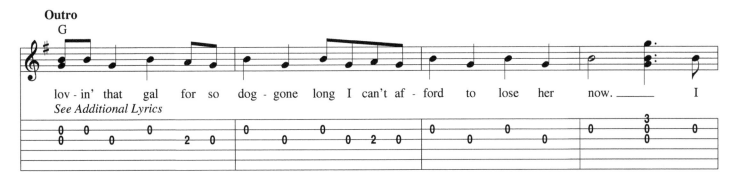

lov - in' that gal for so dog - gone long I can't af - ford to lose her now. ___ I
See Additional Lyrics

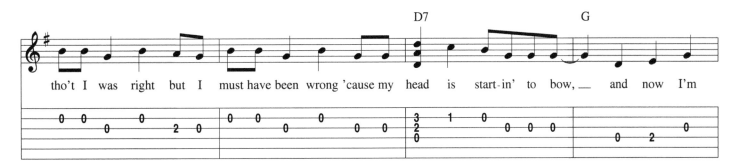

tho't I was right but I must have been wrong 'cause my head is start - in' to bow, ___ and now I'm

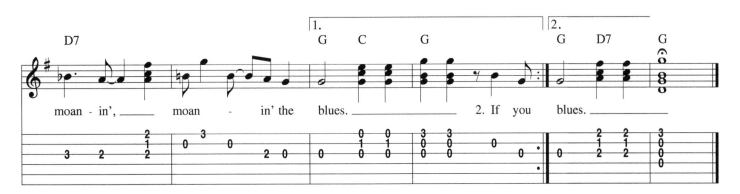

moan - in', ___ moan - in' the blues. ___ 2. If you blues. ___

Additional Lyrics

2. If you want a good gal to stay around
   You got to treat her nice and kind.
   If you do her wrong she'll leave this town
   And you'll almost lose your mind,
   Then you'll be moanin', moanin' the blues.

Bridge Oh baby, baby, baby, honey baby, please come home.
   Your daddy is lonesome and all I do is moan.

Outro I promise you, baby, that I'll be good
   And I'll never be bad no more.
   I'm sittin' here waitin' for you right now
   To walk thru that front door,
   Then I'll stop moanin', moanin' the blues.

My Son Calls Another Man Daddy

Words and Music by Jewell House and Hank Williams

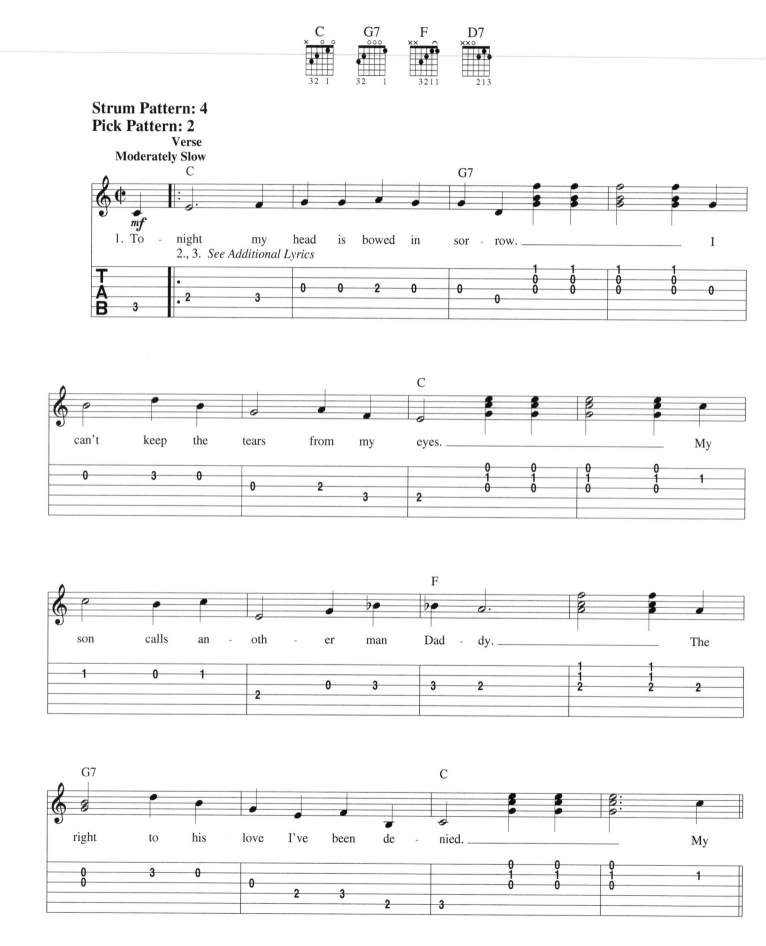

Chorus

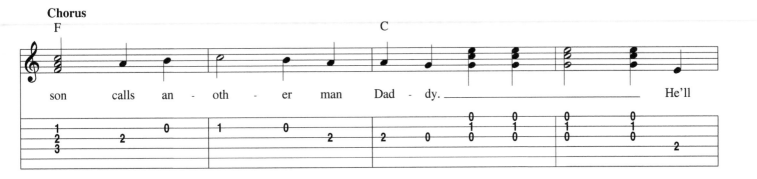

son calls an - oth - er man Dad - dy. _____ He'll

ne'er know my name or my face. _____

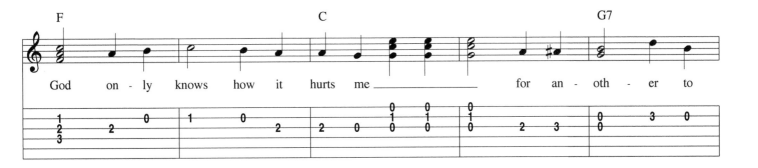

God on - ly knows how it hurts me _____ for an - oth - er to

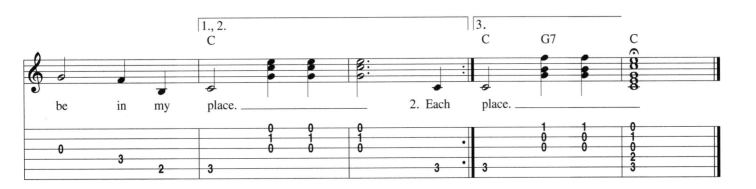

be in my place. _____ 2. Each place. _____

Additional Lyrics

2. Each night I laid there in prison.
   I pictured a future so bright.
   And he was the one ray of sunshine
   That shone through the darkness of night.

3. Today his mother shares a new love.
   She just couldn't stand my disgrace.
   My son calls another man Daddy
   And longs for a love he can't replace.

Ramblin' Man

Words and Music by Hank Williams

did - n't go _____ I b'lieve I'd blow _____ my stack. _____ I

love _____ you ba - by, _____ but you got-ta un - der - stand _____ when the

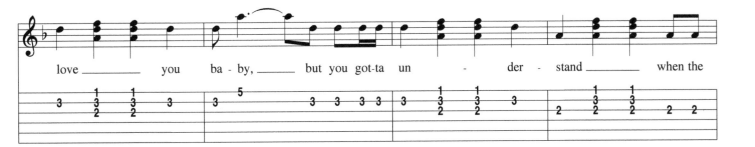

Lord _____ made me, _____ He made a ram - blin' man. _____ 2. Some

ram - blin' man. _____

Additional Lyrics

2. Some folks might say that I'm no good,
   That I wouldn't settle down if I could.
   But when that open road starts to callin' me
   There's somethin' o'er the hill that I gotta see.
   Sometimes it's hard but you gotta understand
   When the Lord made me, He made a ramblin' man.

3. I love to see the towns a passin' by
   And to ride these rails 'neath God's blue sky.
   Let me travel this land from the mountains to the sea
   'Cause that's the life I b'lieve he meant for me.
   And when I'm gone and at my grave you stand,
   Just say God's called home your ramblin' man.

There'll Be No Teardrops Tonight

Words and Music by Hank Williams

Bridge

why _____ should you de - sert me? _____ Are you

See Additional Lyrics

do - ing this for spite? _____ If you

Outro

on - ly want to hurt me, _____ then there'll be _____ no

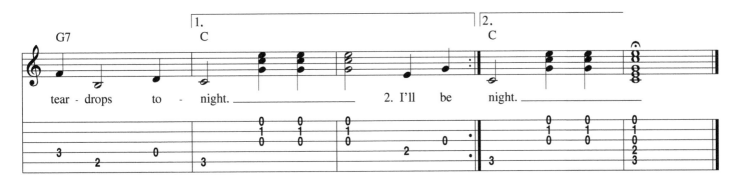

tear - drops to - night. _____ 2. I'll be night. _____

Additional Lyrics

2. I believe that you still love me,
   When you wear your veil of white.
   But you think that you're above me,
   But there'll be no teardrops tonight.

Bridge Shame, oh, shame for what you're doing,
   Other arms will hold you tight.
   You don't care whose life you ruin.

There's a Tear in My Beer

Words and Music by Hank Williams

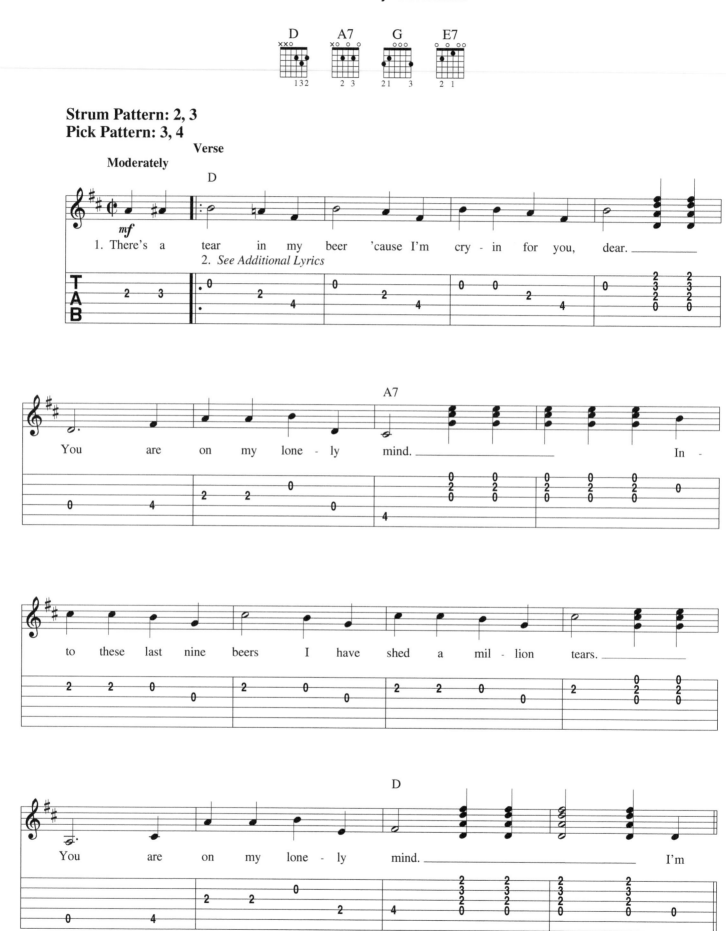

Strum Pattern: 2, 3
Pick Pattern: 3, 4

Bridge

gon - na keep on sit - tin' here un - til I'm pet - ri - fied,

See Additional Lyrics

and then may - be these tears will leave my eyes. There's a

Outro

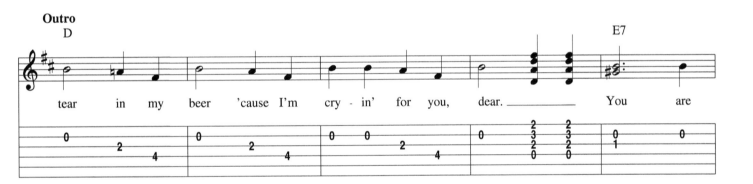

tear in my beer 'cause I'm cry - in' for you, dear. _____ You are

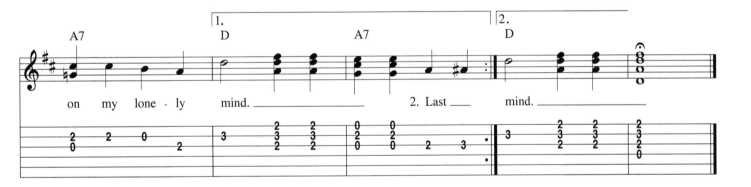

on my lone - ly mind. _____ 2. Last ___ mind. _____

Additional Lyrics

2. Last night I walked the floor,
   And the night before.
   You are on my lonely mind.
   It seems my life is through,
   And I'm so dog-gone blue.
   You are on my lonely mind.

Bridge I'm gonna keep on sittin' here till I can't move a toe.
   And then maybe my heart won't hurt me so.

You Win Again

Words and Music by Hank Williams

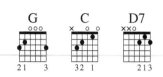

Strum Pattern: 3
Pick Pattern: 3

Verse

Moderately

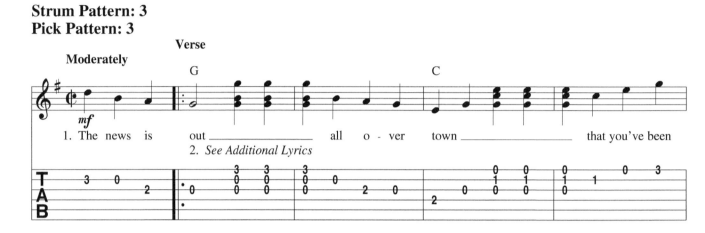

1. The news is out _____ all o - ver town _____ that you've been
2. *See Additional Lyrics*

seen _____ a - run - nin' 'round. _____ I know that

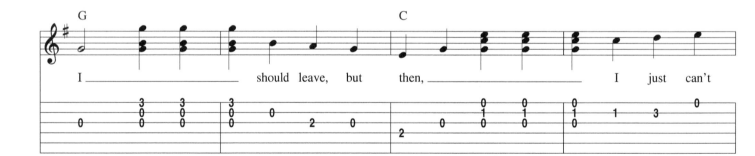

I _____ should leave, but then, _____ I just can't

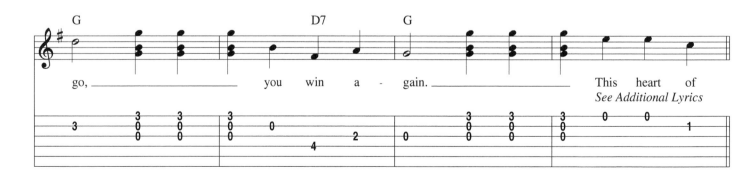

go, _____ you win a - gain. _____ This heart of
See Additional Lyrics

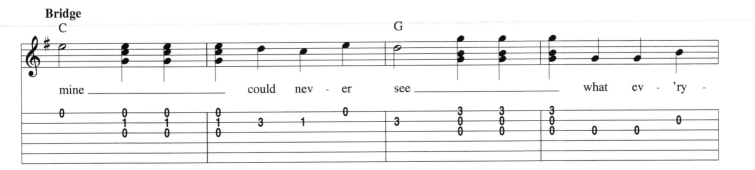

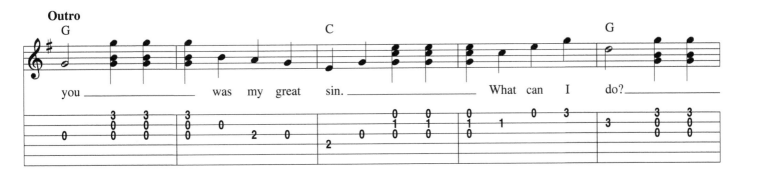

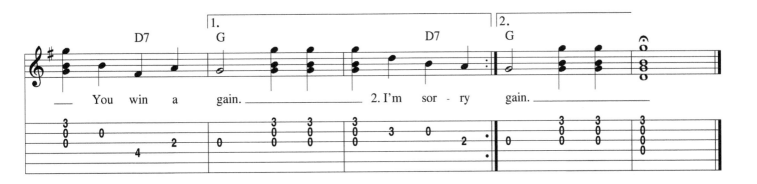

Additional Lyrics

2. I'm sorry for your victim now,
'Cause soon his head like mine will bow.
He'll give his heart, but all in vain.
And someday say, you win again.

Bridge You have no heart, you have no shame.
You take true love and give the blame.

Outro I guess that I should not complain.
I love you still. You win again.

Your Cheatin' Heart

Words and Music by Hank Williams

Strum Pattern: 3
Pick Pattern: 3

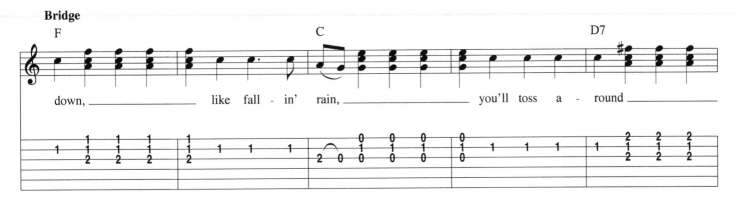

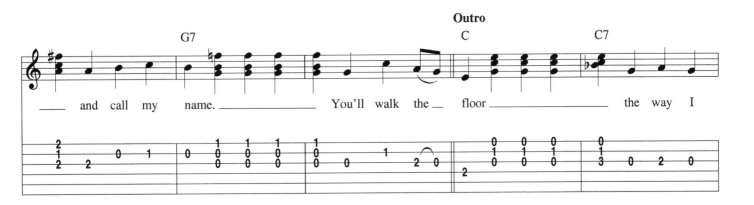

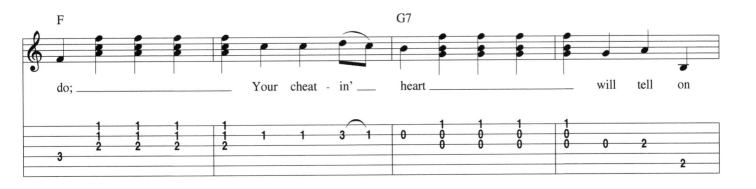

Additional Lyrics

2. Your cheatin' heart will pine someday,
And crave the love you threw away.
The time will come when you'll be blue;
Your cheatin' heart will tell on you.

Move It on Over

Words and Music by Hank Williams

Strum Pattern: 3, 6
Pick Pattern: 5, 6

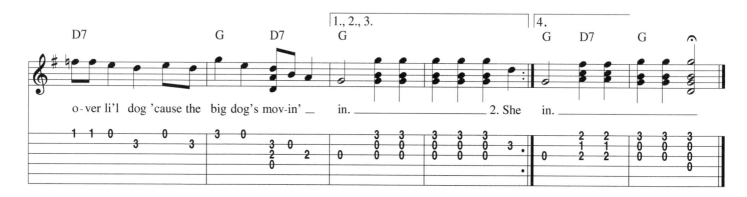

Additional Lyrics

2. She changed the lock on our front door,
   Now my door key don't fit no more,
   So get it on over, (Move it on over.)
   Scoot it on over. (Move it on over.)
   Move over skinny dog 'cause the fat dog's movin' in.

3. This doghouse here is mighty small,
   But it's better than no house at all,
   So ease it on over, (Move it on over.)
   Drag it on over. (Move it on over.)
   Move over old dog 'cause a new dog's movin' in.

4. She told me not to play around,
   But I done let the deal go down,
   So pack it on over, (Move it on over.)
   Tote it on over. (Move it on over.)
   Move over nice dog 'cause a bad dog's movin' in.